HOW TO CONQUER SCIENCE OVERWHELM

BRYAN CHUNG, MD, PhD

Printed in the United States of America
Set in Minion and Morl Sans
Designed by Fredrick Haugen

Image Credits arranged by *source* and (page number):
Unsplash: Aaron Mello (cover); Nick Fewings (9); John Bakator (11); Stefan Steinbauer (14); Yuichi Kageyama (17); Alan Hardman (23); rawpixel (31); Federica Campanaro (32); Ryoki Iwata (38); Derek Thomson (41); Sean Thomas (46); Jamison Riley (48); Fabrizio Verrecchia (51); Artem Bali (53); Robert Collins (55); Eugenio Mazzone (56); Florencia Viadana (60); Joshua Coleman (64), Suzanne D. Williams (68) | *NASA*: Katherine Johnson (20); Astronaut EVA (57) | Rembrandt, *The Storm on the Sea of Galilee* (4) | Edward S. Ellis, *Dewey and Other Naval Commanders* (7) | IKEA (29) | Lily Tomlin courtesy of Tomlin and Wagner Theatricalz (43) | Harry Volkman, WGN Radio & TV (67) | Portrait of Bryan Chung by Marc Betsworth (72)

“You tell me when you want it and where you want it to land, and I’ll do it backwards and tell you when to take off.”

Katherine Johnson, NASA Mathematician

THE ART OF JUMPING SHIP

Assuming you're not the captain, it's easy to abandon ship when the boat is already sinking. In a situation where the alternative is death, there are few, if any, gray areas. There's no art in abandoning a sinking ship. By abandonment, you leave with nothing; you surrender your life to the whim of fate.

Jumping ship, however, is something different. Its origin comes from a time when men were press-ganged (i.e., kidnapped) into military service on the high seas. 'Jumping ship' meant that you didn't show up to the ship you were supposed to be on. Some men passed out from drinking too much while ashore and simply missed their boat. Others jumped ship to avoid the inhumane working conditions imposed on them by the navy.

Essentially, sailors who jumped ship had a positive mindset that there was a better life than impressment. Each person made a conscious decision (well, unconscious if they had passed out) to boldly go to a different destination.

However, jumping ship carried a penalty. If a sailor was caught, punishment ranged from execution to being re-pressed into service. Thus, jumping meant making a calculated decision about the benefits of staying pressed in service versus the benefits of pursuing a different path, despite the risks.

You're here because you need a way to thrive and not just survive. The model of lifelong learning and evidence-based practice in its traditional, school-taught form doesn't work. You've been press-ganged into a framework where you can't keep up. You love your work, yet you feel that you're being asked to ignore your deep, rich experience in order to fit the existing structure. You can't stop working in this framework, but you can't keep working in it either. You'd rather not abandon ship and have nothing. You're looking for a way to jump ship.

The art of jumping ship, therefore, means that we have to know ourselves: what we value, what is important, where our limits lie, and whether our goals are realistic. Jumping ship doesn't mean giving up, or walking away with nothing. It means choosing between investing more energy and resources into something or not. It means jumping to something else where those same energies and resources can be put to better use.

If you are looking to leverage an evidence-based approach to your practice, the art of jumping ship is essential. You have limited time and energy, but we live in an age where access to information is limitless. Learning how to efficiently spend your time is a survival skill. You need to hone your instinct for when you have enough evidence, enough information to act. This is the foundation of good decision-making: knowing when it's time to jump ship.

Dips and dead ends

In his book *The Dip*, Seth Godin talks about the importance of learning when not to start. The Dip is what happens a few days or weeks *after* you start something worthwhile. It's the point of resistance where that new thing doesn't look so shiny anymore. You begin to contemplate the dues that must be paid, the uphill climb, in order to get to a higher level.

Quitting in the Dip is arguably the worst move to make, because your decision will be based entirely on emotion—emotions like pain, fear, and shame. Ultimately, choosing to go through a Dip involves having faith in yourself, and in the system in which you are invested, to see your way through to the reward that lies beyond.

The dead end, however, is that place where it doesn't feel too bad, but it doesn't feel great. Nothing really gets worse, but nothing really gets better. It can be a tolerable place, which is why so many mediocre people end up here. There's nothing wrong with pursuing a dead end. Most popular television entertainment sits comfortably in this spot. It doesn't change your life. It's entertaining. Afterwards, your life is temporarily a little better, or if you watch a show where everyone dies, potentially a little worse.

Winners learn to distinguish between a dead end and a Dip. They quit dead ends before they start. Also, they quit Dips if they assess that the chasm ahead is insurmountable.

There is truth in the saying that, "every no gets you closer to a yes." Learning to say 'no,' in a world filled with bytes of information, helps you weed out that which is not important. Saying 'no' helps you can focus your energy on what *is* important. You're not a sailor abandoning ship with nothing. You're making a choice to spend your resources wisely in spite of the risks.

Everyone has limited time and limited energy and, while hoarding either one isn't helpful, spending them unwisely is also not a good idea. You end up further behind than when you started without much to show for it.

I'm often asked how one can start incorporating research into their life and career; I think respecting that your time is scarce and valuable is the first step towards mastery.

Filtering leads to 'yes'

Using 'no' to effectively leverage research happens in layers, like a water filter. Filters work like a sieve—trapping things that aren't drinkable. The first layer lets everything but the biggest pieces of impurities through; each subsequent layer traps smaller and smaller impurities.

At the first layer of the filter, the speed of water flow is almost normal, but by the time the fluid reaches the last layer, drinkable water only comes out one drip at a time. Pouring in more fluid doesn't speed this process up. No matter how much water you put in a Brita, you don't get a full pitcher of filtered water any faster.

Every layer of a filter needs more processing time, because it takes finer filtration to eliminate ever-smaller impurities, down to things like odor molecules. The filter says 'no' at each layer so that only the important stuff, water, comes out the other end.

Every layer of your research filter needs an uptick in energy, time, and required knowledge. But the ability to filter and say 'no' is an opportunity to use time and energy—that you would have otherwise wasted had you said 'yes'—for something truly worth your attention.

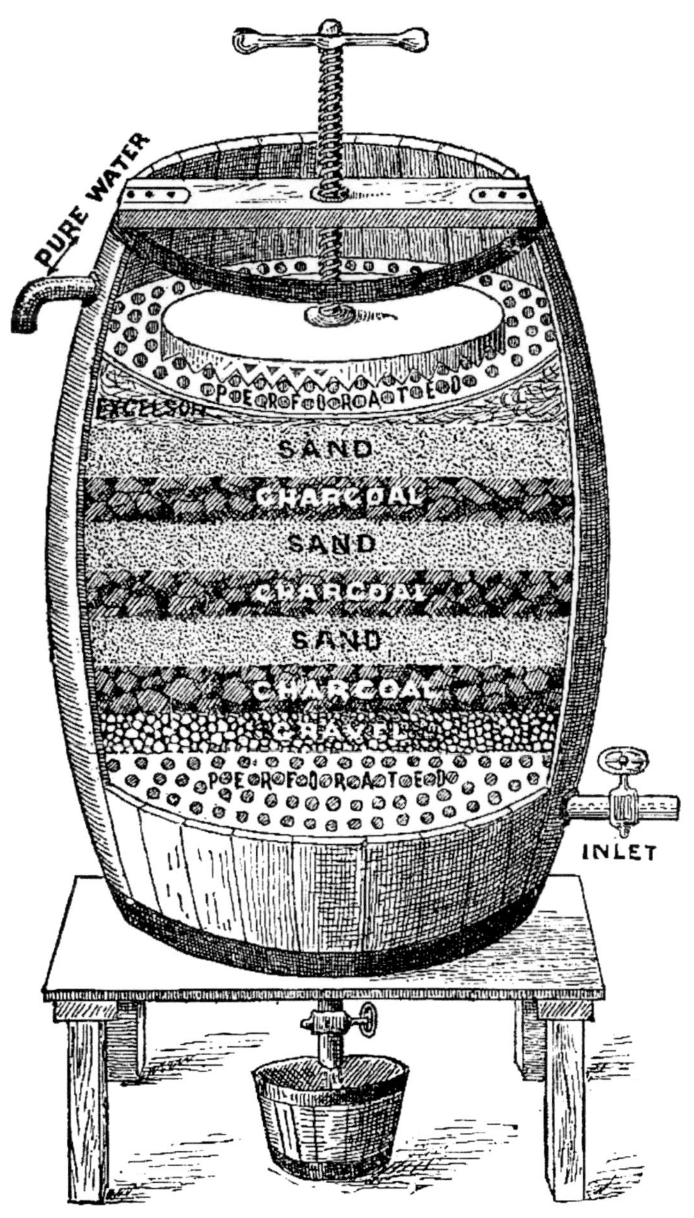
PURE WATER
PERFORATED
EXCELSOR
SAND
CHARCOAL
SAND
CHARCOAL
SAND
CHARCOAL
GRAVEL
PERFORATED
INLET

THE HIDDEN POWER OF BROWSING

There are two kinds of starting when you read something:

- When you read something because it's just passing your field of vision
- When you read something because you have a purpose

In either case, you should always know what you are reading for. In the first case, it's a dead end. Nothing will get much worse, but nothing will get much better. The second case is where the Dip lies (at least, in the beginning).

If you're reading to be entertained or distracted or just to pass time, you don't need to filter anything. It's a dead end in terms of changing what you do, or what you believe. Recognize that what you're doing is being entertained, and move on.

Essentially, you should treat entertainment as fiction. You can get worked up about fiction, but why? For example, whether stories about the Royal Family are true or not have little bearing on your day-to-day life. There's no Dip here. It's a dead end that you choose to engage in for your own reasons. Give yourself permission to be browse-y without a laser-focused goal. But if it pushes your buttons too much, you might want to switch from passive to active reading.

That's not to say that there isn't *any* value in browsing. But browsing is a dead end when it comes to concretely changing the way you behave. Behavior change comes from many places and, sometimes, browsing triggers change which then requires active reading for this reason.

If browsing is a dead end for change, what is it good for?

Browsing is great for increasing your breadth of knowledge. It doesn't result in a great depth of understanding, but it helps you to engage with whomever you are assisting with where they are at in their journey. It also makes you far more interesting to talk to at parties.

A preying mantis sees best when things move; it ignores things that sit still. It has evolved to be this way. You've also evolved, through your education, to follow a certain process to solve problems—to see and fix things in a specific way.

This is great for making interchangeable workers. If everyone thinks in the exactly same way, then you can be replaced (like a cog) when you break down. But rigid thinking is horrible for creativity. What we need now isn't more factory workers, it's more innovation. Browsing outside your area allows you to expand your palette of colors. You gain new ways of seeing—new ways to frame a problem—so that you can solve it differently.

There's a common children's puzzle where an extremely close-up photograph of something is presented with the question, "What is this?" Sometimes you can tell, but in most situations things up close don't trigger patterns until we see the wider picture. Getting too deep into your own groove causes this kind of near-sightedness. Browsing gives us permission to step back and see the larger picture where patterns become evident to form a cohesive picture.

Lastly, browsing builds vocabulary. The more you see certain difficult words, the less unfamiliar they become. If you go through the small amount of work to figure out what they mean, it means having fewer stumbling blocks when you see them again.

QUESTION THE START

Katherine Johnson is a famous mathematician. She was the first African-American woman to attend West Virginia State University. She worked for NASA in an age of segregation and gender discrimination. You may have learned of her amazing story in the film *Hidden Figures*.

When it was time to launch the first American into space, Alan Shepard, Katherine did the calculations *by hand* for the capsule's return trajectory. Asked about the experience afterward she said, "You tell me when you want it and where you want it to land, and I'll do it backwards and tell you when to take off."

What Katherine Johnson understood keenly was a different place to start. She refused to start at the beginning in order to get to the end. She saw past the journey and focused on the place that mattered most—getting the astronaut safely back to Earth. She questioned where to start in order to achieve the most important result.

You do this all the time, just not with astronauts and orbital mechanics. You order a pizza instead of making dinner. When do you order a pizza? You don't *usually* order a pizza halfway through making dinner. You don't gather ingredients together, order pizza, and then put the food you made away.

Sometimes a meal goes horribly wrong; you throw the mess away and order pizza. But, typically, you order pizza *before* you make dinner. You see the most important result—dinner on the table—and start from there, working your way backwards through the possible alternatives. Then you choose.

So why do you order a pizza? You question starting dinner, and when dinner looks like it's just too much to get the most important result—food on the table—you jump ship. You are not choosing to quit, resulting in nothing for dinner. You jump ship. Dinner takes on a different destination and becomes pizza.

When it comes to using research, questioning the start is where you have the opportunity to see the most important result. In this case, it's not dinner but the objective you seek from spending your time on a research topic. Once you know the end, work your way backwards and choose the direction you'll head to get there.

One path leads to a Dip. Quitting after this isn't jumping ship, it's more like abandoning ship. Like realizing that you can't finish making dinner after you've started. You will have squandered resources to end up with, not an alternative, but nothing.

If you've already started making dinner, but realize that you have to stop, then ordering the equivalent of pizza means spending *more* resources going forward than if you had just decided on pizza in the first place. If it feels difficult to make this decision, it's because it's the point in the process where you have the least certainty about the outcome.

If the reason you're reading research is to decide if you should change your behavior—and if behavior change is the most important result—then the following questions need to be taken into consideration before you spend any more time on it skimming.

Would I actually do this?

If the answer is 'no'
then filter it out.
Quit early.

If the answer is 'yes'

You should reflect on:

- What this change is for
- Why you think it is worthy of your attention, your labor, your money, and your spirit

If your answers to these questions don't satisfy you, you shouldn't change your behavior and jump ship on the idea—at least for now.

Why?

Because all meaningful change requires a Dip—that point when an initiative is no longer new enough to be exciting and energizing; instead it's become unpleasant, painful or disruptive. Once you get through the Dip, things get better as you gain confidence and ease. But if you can't articulate *why* you are changing, then chances are you won't make it past the Dip. Abandoning your initiative *now* actually saves time and energy for making changes that really matter to you.

Novelty is a horrible reason to change. "Not right now" is, also, not forever.

If you've ever bought anything requiring complicated assembly from IKEA, you already know what I mean. IKEA looks great in the catalog. It looks beautiful in the store. It's a supreme blend of function and fabulous with products in oddly-shaped boxes. I have no idea how they can engineer a dresser to fit so flat. But I do know that buying furniture from IKEA is going to cause me immense, yet thankfully temporary, pain. That's the Dip.

But before you buy this contraption from hell (that will eventually look awesome in your home), you have to know *why* you're buying it. You need to know where it will go; that it will fit there; that the color will match; and what it's going to be for. You need to know this ahead of time because—once you start assembling it—there's no turning back. Sure, you can return a partially-assembled cabinet to the store. But only if you own a truck. You know there's no way you're getting it back into those flat cardboard boxes again.

If you don't know why you're buying it, then you should not buy it.

That doesn't mean you should never buy it. Maybe you just need to do those measurements one more time. Maybe you need to figure out if another dresser is really what you need. But, until then, you're going to skip the weeping and fetal position that is IKEA furniture assembly.

Otherwise you'll be searching all weekend for that one missing screw thingy, the one requiring a second trip to IKEA only to find out it's not *that* screw thingy, but the *other* screw thingy that you actually needed (seriously, they don't even have Swedish names).

You're going to say 'no' not just to avoid pain, but to say 'yes' to something that has more known value than a whole weekend of assembling one piece of IKEA furniture—something like reading. Or a board game. Or water torture.

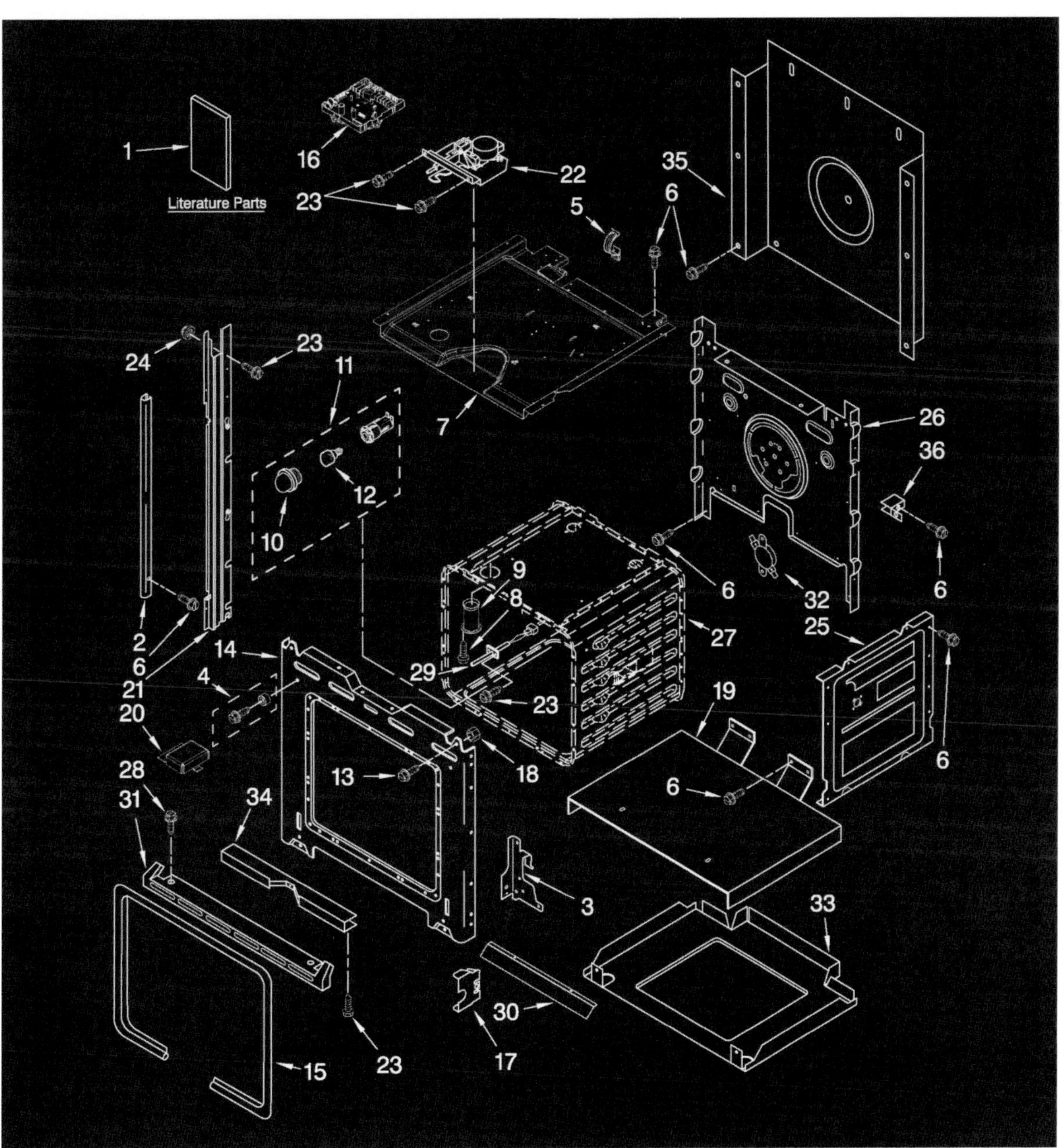

1
Literature Parts
16
22
23
23
35
6
5
24
23
11
7
26
36
12
10
6
32
6
9
8
27
25
2
6
21
14
29
4
23
19
20
18
6
13
28
31
34
3
33
30
23
17
15

How does this relate to everything else that I know?

Any research you read (or read about) is either going to resonate, or not, with how you see the world. If you enjoy a glass of wine every night, a study that says there is no safe amount of alcohol that can be drunk is going to cause some dissonance. Resolving this type of conflict requires digging deeper.

Things that resonate with you should look like they're going to help you do something better. If they merely confirm what you are already doing, filter it out. There's no need to spend time on things that don't *add* to your understanding. It's easy to misinterpret validation (which is just appeasing the fear inside you) for forward motion.

You can recognize dead ends when nothing really changes: nothing worse, but nothing much better. It's a dead end to your time and energy if there isn't something substantial being added to your practice.

Things that don't resonate with you should still look like they're based on some type of shared foundation, unless you're looking to *really* branch out. If you share no basic foundation, filter it out. Because understanding a piece with which you share nothing in common means understanding that foundation first. If you're not prepared to enter into that Dip—the pain of becoming fluent in a new framework—then you will be reading in a void with nothing to anchor the material.

Questioning whether you even allow your attention to be diverted is a critical component to becoming more efficient at using research. Browse heavily, select few. Don't ever read passively unless it's purely for fun.

KNOW WHAT IS IMPORTANT

The worst five words in any science piece are: “They found a significant difference”.

I'm not going to belabor the issue of ‘statistically significant’ versus ‘practically important’. It's been written about already by many others. I've found that, quite often, authors who write about ‘practically important’ don't mention *how* to figure out *what* is practically important.

Statistics are tools. Hammers don't build houses; people build houses with hammers. Statistics don't build importance; people build importance with statistics.

When a piece of research allows statistics to decide what's important, it abandons its responsibility to make sense for you. This typically occurs in areas where measurement is arbitrary (such as a happiness scale). It's why things like ‘effect size’ can be made to seem like they play an integral role in deciphering research.

‘Effect size’ can absolve the author of responsibility and defer what is important to an outside authority—one statistician who said something back in the 1970's in a single book. That person didn't know what *you* would be doing. He didn't know the important factors that come into consideration for your situation—who you would be doing things to, and why.

This isn't to say that properly deployed effect sizes aren't useful, only that using them as the main method to determine what effects are practically meaningful ignores the context in which those effects need to be seen.

Important always depends

I once wrote an article about how 'every little bit' doesn't help. We can get caught up in small changes that don't always lead to making big differences.

One reader wrote back to me that she had a debilitating health issue, and that reading my piece was discouraging because the examples I used to define 'small changes', actually made a big impact on her sense of well-being and ability.

I continue to think about how she reframed my perspective. It drives how I approach my surgical practice in hand surgery. I've found that what one patient thinks is important, another takes for granted. An injured professional musician has different priorities than a grandmother who only wants to enjoy chopping her own vegetables again.

Research can't tell you what's important. It can't tell you whether a statistically significant difference is meaningful. You're the one in charge. You're the one who knows yourself, and the people you serve, best. You're the one who has built a relationship with these people, and who knows their needs and their goals.

Where are the limits?

To reiterate, don't spend time on research that only confirms what you already know.

For you to dedicate time and energy into a paper, it has to add actual value to your behavior. It has to look like it's going to *change* your behavior. However, in order to know what would change your behavior, you have to know where the limits of your knowledge and experience lie. What change is important enough that it would make things better if you adopted it?

One scoop of ice cream is good. Two scoops of ice cream is better. After that, three, four, or five scoops of ice cream doesn't get a whole lot better. But a waffle cone, chocolate sauce, sprinkles... Those make two scoops of ice cream a lot better. It takes something that isn't ice cream to make an important enough change that the two scoops of ice cream becomes better. The limit of ice cream is two scoops (maybe three). So stop wasting your time on the fifth or sixth scoop. Go find a topping.

Knowing what's important helps you weed out papers that aren't relevant to the people you are trying to serve as well as papers that aren't relevant to *you*. If you don't know what an important difference is, then you're letting someone else—someone who *doesn't* know your clients and practice best—decide what's important.

You're letting a stranger decide your destiny.

FIND THE QUESTION

You've decided to start. You know what's important. The first part of the Dip is identifying your research question.

Finding the research question helps you understand the critical components of the study, and whether or not you should spend the time to go through the results in detail.

In an abstract, you should be able to find:

1. Who exactly was studied
2. What was done to them, or what they did to themselves
3. What the researchers measured afterwards

If you can't discern the question from the abstract, and you really want to keep going, then you must be able to find it somewhere in the introduction and methods of the paper. But whether you spend this extra energy depends on how interested you are. Choose wisely.

Why does there have to be such clarity?

When you call a customer service line, you get one of two representatives—the one who can fix your problem, or the one who has to refer you to the next person (who may, or may not, be able to fix your problem). You can usually figure out, within 30 seconds of describing your issue, which one they are. The person who can fix your problem will repeat, in their own words, what is occurring and suggest a solution, while the representative who starts with "Did you turn it off and turn it back on again?" is somebody who will eat away at your soul.

One person is going to waste your time. The other person fixes your problem.

A study that cannot clearly articulate the question "What is it for?" reflects the fuzzy thinking of authors who don't know the purpose of their research. Wishy-washy objectives lead to wishy-washy data and conclusions. These type of muddled conclusions may be useful if you're a researcher looking to clear up the wishy or washy, but they don't fix problems. Remember: you are trying to fix a problem, not create knowledge about new ones.

Where are the limits?

Finding the three elements in an abstract allows you answer the questions:

1. Does who they studied match or closely resemble who I'm interested in helping with this? If they're different, how different? If they're different enough, you can say no.

2. Does what they did to the people in the study match, or closely resemble what I'm thinking of doing, or what I can do? If they're different, how different? If they're different enough, you can say no.

3. Does what they measured match or closely resemble something I'm interested in making better? If they're different, how different? If they're different enough, you can say no.

What's different enough?

In *The Matrix* a young boy taught Neo that there is no spoon.

"Do not try and bend the spoon. That's impossible. Instead, only try to realize the truth... There is no spoon. Then you will see that it is not the spoon that bends, it is only yourself."

In research, there is no universal threshold of 'enough'. There is only what you know is 'enough'. 'Different enough' comes from your deep knowledge of the people you serve, and the rich experience you've accumulated from years of practice. It also comes from knowing where your knowledge runs out. 'Enough' changes with every situation. 'Enough' changes as your experience changes. 'Different enough' happens when you convince yourself it's enough.

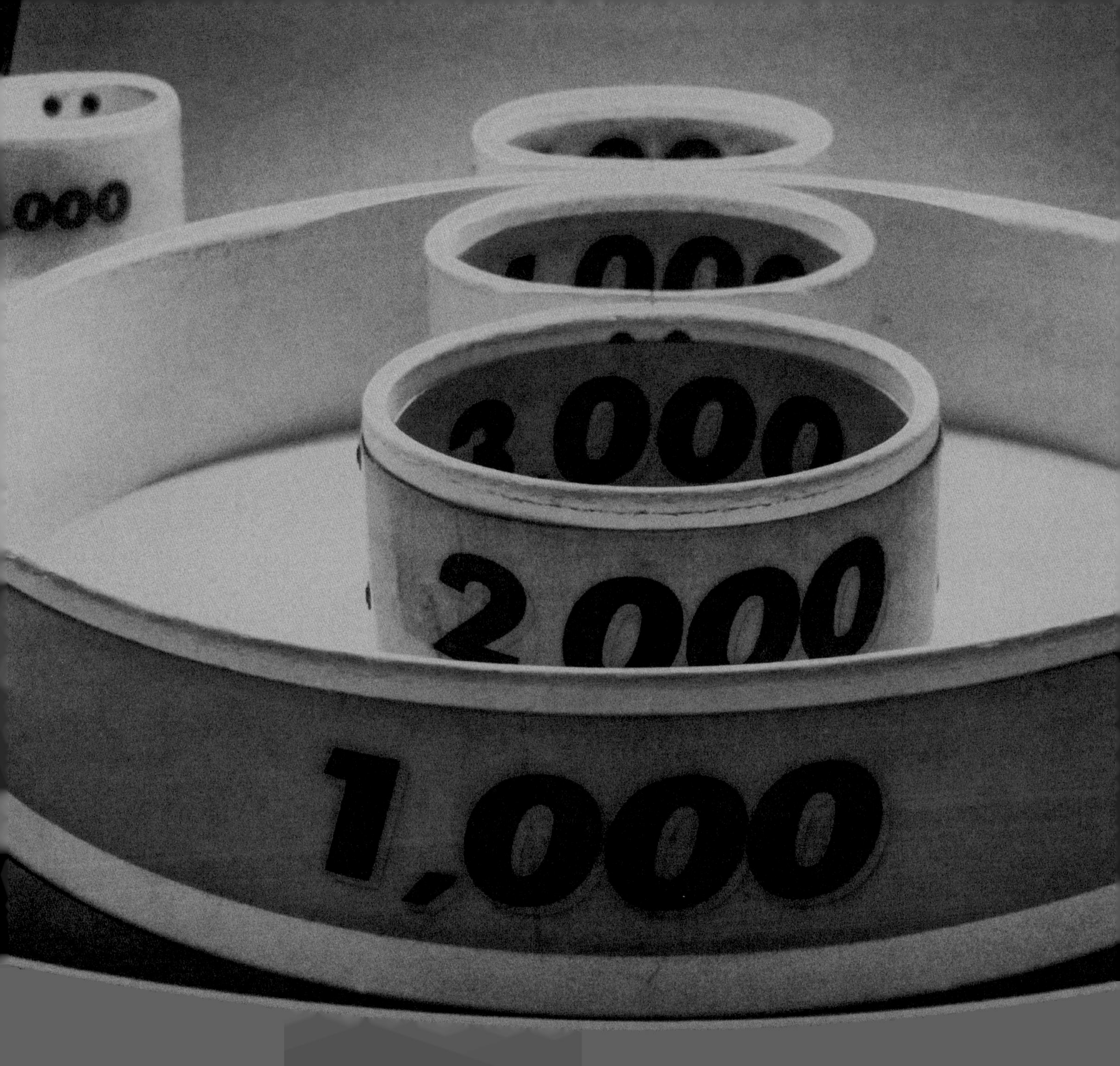
3,000
2,000
1,000

SKILL IS BETTER THAN NUMBERS

The most common barrier people present to me when confronted with reading research is their aversion to statistics. They'll shrug their shoulders and say "I'm not good at statistics."

At the root of this statement are two things:

1. Buying into a broken framework
2. The fear that comes from buying into a broken framework

What does it mean to 'not be good' at something?

When I was a kid, I couldn't catch. I mean I couldn't catch anything—a ball, a set of keys, a candy bar. Everything ended up on the ground, or it bounced off of my outstretched hand, careened wildly into the air, *then* ended up on the floor.

Play the piano? No problem. I was a little Mozart. But hand-eye coordination in a sport? No way. Everyone gets teased for something. Not catching was one of my status-drainers.

This got so bad that, by the time I was in high school, I stopped trying to catch at all. If I sensed someone was going to toss something my way, I'd rush over to stop them. I'd bridge the distance myself to pick up the thing. I feared the judgement of new friends if they ever found out I was a horrible catcher. What I didn't know was: I'd grown out of it. Actually, I could catch. The other, more important, thing that I didn't realize was—no one cared either way.

I bought into a broken framework at an early age that catching was important, and that I sucked at it. I continued to believe this long after I had improved my ability. I continued to believe in a broken framework long after it was relevant.

The fear

The fear, of course, is about being wrong. The fear (or the shame) is that people will think less of you. Not *if* you are wrong, but *when* you are wrong. This is the story we tell ourselves to stay safe. Never trying to catch means you will never be embarrassed about missing.

Tests and certifications are just the opposite. They give us permission. They give us false confidence that we 'understand' something. But the type of learning needed to pass a test is not the same thing as *actual* understanding. The proof that this is false confidence is because almost everyone who says, "I'm not good at statistics" has passed at least one course on statistics.

The lie you are fed

The more you buy into statistics being the critical link in a study, the less power you will feel (and have) over your destiny.

From the very get-go of introducing research to students, the traditional college/university education system says "You start by learning statistics". Most undergraduate science programs do not have structured courses on the skills of research interpretation beyond statistics. You are expected to acquire these skills by osmosis. The thought is that, by learning about your field, you will naturally gain these skills. Yet statistics aren't natural; you can't gain them naturally. It's the same as expecting you to intuitively learn a new language. It's not natural. And statistics is essentially a new language.

So what does this signal tell you? What does the fact that a course on statistics exists but a course about all of the other aspects of research interpretation typically does not?

It broadcasts the message that the limiting factor to you understanding research lies in statistics; that the keyholder of scientific knowledge is the one who is 'good at statistics'.

To be 'not good at statistics' requires that you believe a framework where statistics are the root of science understanding—followed by the belief that you must be 'good enough' at statistics to deserve to interact with science in the first place.

But it's a broken framework.

It's a lie that you have been taught (inadvertently, I'm sure). As a result, you maintain this limitation unconsciously. The lie keeps you safe. But it also keeps you in your place.

You're good enough

The lie you are fed becomes the story you believe.

It's rare for a study to fall down on statistics alone. Is it necessary to grasp some of the numbers to fully comprehend a study? Yes. But you almost never need to understand them to *filter* a study. And you definitely don't need to understand them in their entirety to start the filtering process, or even to start reading.

There's no one course on statistics that makes you 'good at statistics'. There's a whole branch of mathematics called statistics. What you need is practice.

Comfort in catching objects comes from missing less. Developing the skill to catch involves catching slow-moving things, then progressing to faster-moving things. Step by step toward your chosen end.

You know enough to start. You know enough to start missing. You just need someone who isn't whipping fastballs at you right away. And you need people around you whose opinion of you doesn't depend on whether you catch or miss.

The reason why in-depth statistical knowledge is the least of your worries at the filtering stage is because the research question is what dictates the statistics being used. Statistics fall down when the authors don't have a clear idea of what is the question *they* wanted to answer.

So, if you find that you can't clearly identify a research question, then the statistics really don't matter. Instead it's likely that the study doesn't get at the question in a focused enough manner to help you.

Most of the time, a clear research question leads to very clear statistics. Appearances matter, and lack of focus often leads to poor clarity of presentation. If the question seems simple and the statistics are ridiculously complicated, something is wrong. Either you've identified the wrong question, or there's something new you need to learn.

Likewise when the question appears quite complicated and the statistics are simple, that's also indicative of a potential mismatch. Being able to identify this is the first skill you need to see statistics, and your relationship with them, differently.

Statistics are tools. Skill is better.

Yes, you eventually need to learn the lingo. Yes, you will have to delve deeper if you are serious about leveraging this tool beyond filtering. But you don't have to learn it all at once. It's okay to approach each new area of inquiry as you need it.

You can read every word of all of the instruction manuals for all of the possible tools. But what you really need to do is build a bookshelf. Statistics are tools. Skill is better.

Change your story. Change how you see.

You are enough.

END WITH THE QUESTION

Now that you've done the reading, you can't *undo* the reading. Now that you've spent the time to go through a Dip, you've attained a new understanding—you can't go back. What you control is whether it becomes a part of who you are or what you do. The last step in the filtering process is deciding whether you want to let this information in.

Did the paper do what it said it would do?

Searching for the question involves looking in up to four places: the introduction, the methods, the statistics, and the conclusion. These don't always match up. Ultimately, the question that's answered is the one that's responded to by the methods—regardless of what is explicitly stated anywhere else.

Conflicts between the question and the answer indicate the author's own poor sense of clarity or understanding. And, sometimes, something is just plain fishy. When a paper doesn't do what it claimed it would do, it's a sign to proceed with caution.

We like to think that we make decisions based on what we *know*, but the reality is that the biggest parts of our decisions are made by how we *feel*. What we know shapes how we feel, but it's very difficult for knowledge to override feeling. When you get enough good practice, papers that don't deliver on their question start to 'feel' wrong before you know they are wrong.

Are you satisfied that you spent this time, or not?

Satisfaction comes from expectations being met. That's why you can feel satisfied after eating at McDonald's but not satisfied after eating at a fancy restaurant. A fancy restaurant sets a high bar. If it fails to meet that level of service, taste, presentation, smell, cleanliness, decor, wine list, or value, then satisfaction goes down.

McDonald's doesn't pretend to be something it's not. It's cheap, fast food. Your expectation is low. If it tastes pretty good and fills you up, that's potentially higher than you expect from McDonald's. Service, presentation, decor… they don't even register on the scale of expectation here. So your satisfaction can be pretty good or even high.

Likewise, feeling satisfied or unsatisfied with a study has to with the expectation that you set based on what you read, and whether or not that expectation was met. You paid for the study with your time. You expect a certain value. This isn't the same as disagreeing with a study's conclusions—unless your goal is to be right, then you should expect a lot of dissatisfaction.

Most people would say that they expect to come away from a paper knowing something they didn't know before *that they can use in their practice.*

It's unsatisfying to put time into a paper only to find that you are *more* justified in doing what you're already doing. That's why you jump ship as soon as you realize this is going on.

Resonance happens when two things are tuned and aligned with one another. When one thing vibrates—even though it not touching the other object—it causes the other to vibrate. To achieve true resonance means that the alignment has to be close to perfect. Being off, even just slightly, doesn't cut it.

Dissonance, however, comes from not being aligned at all. In the case of research studies, this manifests as disagreement. Disagreement happens because the findings are opposite to what you know, or what you *thought* you knew. Sometimes, the findings are opposite to what you are *doing*—posing a serious threat to your sense of self and identity as a practitioner.

Just as 'what is important' changes with context, research that resonates with us for one context might not resonate in another. Thus, when something feels dissonant, it's important to explore *why* you feel that way. Is this context-specific? Does it threaten the way you see the world? If so, do you share enough foundation with the new information to see why you might need to question the way you see the world?

Try this: don't reject the answer; reject the question itself.

How does that feel?

If rejecting the question feels wrong (because the question is worthy), then you have a problem with the answer. It's harder to justify throwing away a worthy finding solely because you don't like the answer.

"Does this duck come in green?" is a worthy question.

"No, it only comes in yellow" might not be the answer you like, but it doesn't change the fact that you're not getting a green duck.

'No' gets you closer to 'yes'.

But every 'yes' involves saying 'no' to other things.

Yin and Yang—no light without darkness. When you say 'yes', you should remember the 'no' (singular or plural) that comes along with it.

When the weatherperson is wrong, you don't allow their view of how the weather was supposed to be dictate how you spend your day. If it's warm enough to wear shorts, you're going to wear shorts. Despite their being wrong today, you're probably going to check the weather again for tomorrow. It's okay to say "Not today," instead of "Not ever."

Every decision you make is like a different day.

Saying 'no' isn't forever. Context can change, even if research doesn't. Evidence-based practice is optimal when you think of it as a true interplay. When you use the lens of your own experience—and the the lens of the person you're serving—and apply it to the research, you see what looks back at you. But, also, the reverse is true. You can employ the lens of the research to examine your experience.

Tuning your lens in both directions is how you get better and more efficient at the process. And learning how to say "No, not now" is a really good start.

HEAVY SNOW
85
SEVERE WEATHER
90°
HOT AND HUMID

EPILOGUE: TOWARDS A ‘YES’

Where this journey continues is turning 'no, not now' into 'now now now'. It's a change of two letters. It's a change of two letters that our minds will try to avoid at all costs.

The key is not to fight ourselves, but to find the path around the resistance. We must see differently to transform 'no' into 'now'.

Learning how to say 'no', and how to jump ship opens up space. It clears the path for you to say 'yes'. People who jumped ship didn't fight the press gangs, they left behind the ways of their old life—including all of the social structures that came with it—and stepped boldly onto the shore to cut their own path. That doesn't necessarily mean they stopped doing what they did in their old lives. They just did it from a new mental space, in a different light. In the sunlight of 'yes'.

When you're ready to see where 'yes' takes you, you are prepared for a journey to the edge of knowledge. From that cliff, you can see—not only what isn't there—but what is present.

It involves a different journey, another way of seeing. It can transform the relationship you have with science. It's not for everyone. Sometimes 'no' is enough. Jumping ship looks like it's saying 'no', but it's 'no' to a life of servitude and lost causes. Jumping ship is all about saying 'no' in order to say 'yes' to greater things.

Getting to the edge of knowledge is a journey that I refer to as Critical Mass.

About the author

Bryan Chung is a methodologist who improves people's relationship with science. He is a plastic/hand surgeon and PhD research designer. The biggest compliment he's ever received was from his mentor while in residency. After winning the award for Best Paper by a Resident at a worldwide congress in plastic surgery, his professor said, "You deserve this award because, after four years, I finally understand what you're talking about." Bryan has been getting better at helping people understand what he's talking about since. He won't shut up about evidence-based practice, and sometimes is invited to not shut up about it by important people and institutions globally.

He is the advice columnist behind Dear Doctor Ninja, deardoctor.ninja

Learn more about how you can say 'yes' to greater things at criticalmass.ninja

Made in the USA
Monee, IL
10 September 2019